nF419973

Islam Between Universalism and Sectarianism

Author S. Norman Gee

Universalism and Secterianism
in Islam

3

3

Table of Contents

Notion Statement*

Islam, as established by the Prophet Muhammad, rests upon three core principles: the oneness of God, the prophecy of Muhammad and all preceding prophets, and the Imamah, divinely assigned to Imam Ali, as declared at Ghadir Khumm. Furthermore, Allah exclusively endowed the celestial purified with the knowledge of the Quran, as affirmed in Ayat al-Tathir (Quran 33:33): 'Indeed, Allah desires to keep away impurities from you, O people of the House, and to purify you thoroughly.' This purification designates them as uniquely fit to guide believers and interpret the divine message. Orders and teachings from these divinely purified figures carry universal appeal and acceptance. However, the Saqifah leadership, beginning with Umar's statement, 'The Book of Allah is enough for us,' not only rejected this divine designation but also undermined the entire prophecy. Surah Al-Hujurat further condemns both Abu Bakr and Umar, asserting that 'they do not comprehend,' highlighting a divine rejection of their authority. Their actions, such as burning the Prophet's Sunnah, prohibiting its discussion, and jailing narrators, exemplify this opposition. Additionally, they appointed mostly non-Arabs loyal to them to interpret the Quran, distancing the faith from its prophetic roots and fostering divergent interpretations that fragmented Islam. This thesis investigates how these sectarian actions diverged from the Prophet's universal vision, reshaping Islamic authority, tradition, and interpretation."

Reasons Supporting the Exclusivity and Inherent Purity of Ahl al-Bayt in Ayat al-Tathir (Quran 33:33) Verse of Purification (Ayat al-Tathir):

"إِنَّمَا يُرِيدُ اللَّهُ لِيُذْهِبَ عَنكُمُ الرِّجْسَ أَهْلَ الْبَيْتِ وَيُطَهِّرَكُمْ تَطْهِيرًا"

("Indeed, Allah desires to keep impurities away from you, O People of the House, and to purify you thoroughly.")

Positioning of Ayat al-Tathir:

- Relevant phrase: "إِنَّمَا يُرِيدُ اللَّهُ" (Indeed, Allah desires).

Linguistic Interpretation:

- إِنَّمَا (innama) indicates exclusivity, emphasizing that Allah's desire is solely directed toward the purification of Ahl al-Bayt, without extending this to others.
- يُرِيدُ (yuridu) in present tense suggests an ongoing, continuous divine intention.
  - **Explanation:** Positioned as an interjection within verses addressed to the Prophet's wives, this phrase shifts the focus entirely to Ahl al-Bayt, indicating their unique and divinely favored status.

Conditional Familial Status of the Wives:

- ○ ***Relevant phrase:*** "عَنكُمُ الرِّجْسَ أَهْلَ الْبَيْتِ" *(to keep impurity away from you, O People of the House).*

- ○ *Linguistic Interpretation:*

  - ▪ عَنكُمُ *(ankum) signifies "from you," indicating a spatial or metaphorical distance between Ahl al-Bayt and any impurity.*

  - ▪ الرِّجْسَ *(al-rijs) refers specifically to impurity, in a moral, spiritual, or physical sense, emphasizing the absolute nature of the purity intended.*

- ○ ***Explanation:*** *This phrase is directed solely at Ahl al-Bayt. The conditional nature of the familial status of wives, which ends upon divorce or death, contrasts with Ahl al-Bayt's perpetual, divinely appointed association.*

Restricted Scope of the Term "Family" in Ayat al-Tathir:

Relevant phrase: "أَهْلَ الْبَيْتِ" *(People of the House).*

- ○ *Linguistic Interpretation:*
  - ▪ أَهْلَ *(ahl) implies intimate or close kinship but is context-dependent.*

- ▪ الْبَيْتِ *(al-bayt, "the house") has a strong association with the Prophet's immediate family, referring specifically to those closest to him by blood and divine mission.*

  - ○ ***Explanation:*** *The term "Ahl al-Bayt" in this context is restricted to the Prophet's immediate family members, not extending to distant relatives. This exclusivity is supported by Hadith al-Kisa' and the use of innama in the verse.*

Continuous Divine Will for Purification:

  - ○ *Relevant phrase:* "يُرِيدُ اللَّهُ" *(Allah desires).*

  - ○ ***Linguistic Interpretation:***

    - ▪ يُرِيدُ *(yuridu) is in the present tense, indicating that Allah's will for purification is not a single action but a sustained and continuous intention.*

  - ○ ***Explanation:*** *Allah's will for Ahl al-Bayt's purification is uninterrupted, suggesting a permanent divine safeguard that establishes their enduring purity and role as guides for the Muslim community.*

Divine Immunity from Impurity (رجس) from Creation:

Relevant phrase: "لِيُذْهِبَ عَنكُمُ الرِّجْسَ" *(to keep impurity away from you).*

Linguistic Interpretation:

- لِيُذْهِبَ *(li-yudhhiba) implies an act of keeping or preventing rather than removing, which would suggest impurity was never present.*

- الرِّجْسَ *(al-rijs) denotes impurity of the most severe kind, covering spiritual, moral, and physical defilement.*

- **Explanation:** *This construction implies that Ahl al-Bayt were created in a state of purity where impurity could not reach them from the start. The word order emphasizes that they are immune to impurity, rather than needing to be purified from it.*

Protection Against Slander and Hypocrisy:

- Relevant phrase: "لِيُذْهِبَ عَنكُمُ الرِّجْسَ" *(to keep impurity away from you).*

- *Linguistic Interpretation:*

  - *This phrase can be interpreted as a statement to believers to disregard any negative claims about Ahl al-Bayt, aligning with Quranic guidance in*

Surah Al-Hujurat against accepting slander or accusations without proof.

- o **Explanation:** *Believers are instructed to see any accusations against Ahl al-Bayt as hypocritical, as their divine purity inherently makes them trustworthy and upright, exempting them from faults that might be attributed to others.*

Enduring Theological Conflict:

Relevant phrase: "يُطَهِّرَكُمْ تَطْهِيرًا" (and to purify you thoroughly).

- o *Linguistic Interpretation:*

  - يُطَهِّرَكُمْ *(yutahirakum) in the present tense suggests an ongoing, reinforcing process of purification.*

  - تَطْهِيرًا *(tathīran, a verbal noun) emphasizes completeness and depth, reinforcing that Ahl al-Bayt's purity is unbreakable and comprehensive.*

- o **Explanation:** *This thorough and sustained purification sets Ahl al-Bayt apart as spiritually untouchable. It creates a fundamental divide between divinely sanctioned leadership, represented* *by Ahl al-Bayt, and political power struggles, leading to historical and theological conflicts within the Muslim world.*

Concluding Statement on the Universality of Ayat al-Tathir:

Ayat al-Tathir stands as a profound testament to the universal essence of Islam, represented by the divinely purified Ahl al-Bayt, who embody the pure, unchanging reality of divine guidance. In a world marked by division and competing interpretations, this verse symbolizes the singular truth of Islam—a truth as indivisible as Allah Himself. Through Ahl al-Bayt, Ayat al-Tathir extends a call to believers worldwide to seek peace, unity, and authentic knowledge, untainted by worldly impurities or factionalism. It serves as a guiding light, affirming the oneness of divine reality, bound in the purity and continuity of Islam's truest message.

Accountability and Message of Ayat al-Hujurat Verses 1-4:

Respect *for* Divine Authority in the Context of Universalism and Sectarianism

1. Admonition Against Acting Ahead of Allah and His Messenger

- o **Verse 1:** *"O you who have believed, do not proceed ahead of Allah and His Messenger, and fear Allah. Indeed, Allah is Hearing and Knowing."*

- o ***Core Message:*** *This verse emphasizes the foundational principle of deference to divine authority, a core element of Islam's universal mission. Believers are called to unity under Allah's guidance; any attempt to assert personal authority or judgment independently disrupts this divine order and fosters division, which can lead to sectarianism.*

- o ***Accountability:*** *By setting Allah's guidance as the absolute, this verse underscores that universal submission to divine will prevents the ego-driven divisions that lead to sectarian fragmentation, urging believers to prioritize unity and accountability.*

2. *Warning Against Raising Voices Above the Prophet's*

- o ***Verse 2:*** *"O you who have believed, do not raise your voices above the voice of the Prophet or speak loudly to him as you do to one another, lest your deeds become worthless while you perceive not."*

- o ***Core Message:*** *This verse underscores the universal respect due to the Prophet's authority. Elevating one's voice above the Prophet's signifies an attempt to assert personal importance, a transgression that introduces division and reflects a break from Islam's universal values of unity and humility.*

o ***Accountability and Unique Nature of the Incident:*** *Here, we see a shift to past actions with "those who raise their voices," suggesting that this incident was unique and unrepeatable due to the absence of the Prophet and those specific actors. This judgment, therefore, is singular, like that of Abu Lahab, with a curse that remains as long as the Quran lives in the hearts of believers. Such judgment underscores that sectarianism often emerges from self-assertion, challenging the Prophet's voice, which serves as the unifying guide in Islam.*

3. Commendation of Those Who Lower Their Voices in Reverence

o ***Verse 3 :*** *"Indeed, those who lower their voices before the Messenger of Allah — they are the ones whose hearts Allah has tested for righteousness; for them is forgiveness and a great reward."*

o *Core Message: This verse sets forth the universal value of humility, with Allah declaring those who lower their voices as having been tested and found righteous. The present tense in "those who lower" indicates an enduring quality for those who embody humility, aligning them with Islam's universal essence and standing in contrast to sectarian attitudes born from arrogance.*

- o **Accountability:** *Those who respect the Prophet's voice demonstrate devotion to Islam's universal principles, meriting forgiveness and divine reward. This judgment, unlike others, is unique in its endorsement of those who value the unity and harmony at the heart of Islam.*

4. Rebuke of Impatience and Lack of Understanding

- o **Verse 4:** *"Indeed, those who call you from behind the chambers — most of them do not use reason."*

- o **Core Message:** *This verse rebukes those who called out impatiently to the Prophet, reflecting a lack of understanding of the Prophet's status and the universal principle of respectful approach. The critique underscores that disregard for prophetic decorum reveals an absence of insight into the unity and respect that Islam requires, and it directly challenges the self-centered tendencies that can lead to sectarian impulses.*

- o **Accountability:** *Allah's judgment that they "do not use reason" suggests that sectarian attitudes are often rooted in impatience, self-interest, and a failure to grasp Islam's universal call for unity and reverence for prophetic authority.*

Structured List of Hadiths and Tafsir References on Raising Voices Over the Prophet.

1. Hadiths Explicitly Naming Both Abu Bakr and Umar

- ### *Sahih al-Bukhari*
  - *Volume 6, Book of Tafsir, Hadith 4845:* *This hadith recounts both Abu Bakr and Umar raising their voices in the presence of the Prophet, leading to the revelation of Ayat al-Hujurat as a divine command to show reverence.*

- ### *Musnad Ahmad ibn Hanbal*
  - *Volume 3, Hadith 157:* *This narration describes a disagreement between Abu Bakr and Umar in the Prophet's presence, where their voices were raised, prompting Allah's directive for humility.*

- ### *Tafsir al-Tabari*
  - *Jami' al-Bayan fi Ta'wil al-Quran (Volume 22, Page 178-180):* *In his commentary on Ayat al-Hujurat, Tabari names both Abu Bakr and Umar explicitly, noting that the revelation was a reprimand directed at their conduct in the Prophet's presence.*

2. Hadiths Naming Only One of the Two:

- ***Sahih Muslim***
  - ***Book 44, Hadith 4227:*** *This narration focuses on Umar raising his voice, mentioning him specifically while other companions remain unnamed, marking a partial but significant account of the event.*

- ***Tafsir Ibn Kathir***
  - ***Tafsir of Surah Al-Hujurat (Volume 7, Pages 366-368):*** *Ibn Kathir references Umar in his interpretation of Ayat al-Hujurat, discussing the severity of raising one's voice over the Prophet and emphasizing the respect required.*

3. Hadiths Keeping the Perpetrators Unnamed:

- ***Sunan Abu Dawood***
  - ***Volume 5, Book of Manners, Hadith 4855:*** *This hadith generalizes the action, mentioning "some companions" without specifying names, which dilutes individual accountability.*

- ***Sunan an-Nasa'i***
  - ***Volume 6, Book of Etiquette, Hadith 9135:*** *Refers to "those who were with the Prophet" speaking loudly, presented as a collective issue rather than a specific fault of prominent figures.*

- ***Tafsir al-Qurtubi***
  - ***Al-Jami' li Ahkam al-Quran (Volume 16, Pages 309-310):*** *Qurtubi uses broad terms like "some people" when describing those who raised their voices, lessening the focus on specific individuals and generalizing the incident.*

Historical Context on Hadith Compilation and Documentation

These narrations were recorded approximately 200 years after the Prophet's death, following the burning of original documentation of the Sunnah. This delay and the reliance on oral transmission led to variations across sources, some of which either obscure or generalize details, such as the identities of prominent figures involved. This narrative shift suggests that later compilations may have attempted to minimize the incident's impact by presenting it as a general behavioral lapse rather than a significant transgression by specific individuals.

Conclusion on Ayat al-Hujurat Verses 1-4: A Call to Universal Respect for Divine Authority

The opening verses of Surah Al-Hujurat deliver a powerful, singular judgment regarding respect and reverence toward the Prophet. They establish the boundaries of true faith, where universalism is defined by unwavering adherence to prophetic guidance. The specific condemnation of those who raised their voices above the Prophet's serves as an eternal reminder of the consequences of overstepping divine authority. This unique incident—unrepeatable in history—remains a warning against sectarian tendencies rooted in self-assertion and disregard for prophetic sanctity.

Through this passage, the Quran delineates a universal principle: only those who embody humility and restraint in the presence of Allah's Messenger align with Islam's true message. In contrast, those driven by self-interest or arrogance stray into sectarianism, fragmenting the unity essential to the faith. By embedding this judgment within the Quran, Allah reinforces the timeless necessity of reverence toward prophetic authority, preserving a lesson that echoes through generations.

The Incident of Ghadir Khumm:
Establishing Leadership and Authority!

1. Context and Strategic Location of Ghadir Khumm

- **Date and Location:** *The event at Ghadir Khumm took place on the 18th of Dhu al-Hijjah in the 10th year of Hijra, following the Prophet's final pilgrimage. Ghadir Khumm is a stream located in the desert,* *traditionally a gathering point where travelers would meet before taking their separate routes to different regions.*

- ***Strategic Location:*** *Ghadir Khumm is a stream located in the desert, a customary meeting point where travelers would gather before taking their separate routes to different regions. By choosing this location, the Prophet ensured that the largest possible assembly of people witnessed the declaration.*

- ***Significance of Location:*** *Divine Necessity of Appointment for Completion of Religion. This gathering at a major crossroads highlights the deliberate choice to announce Imam Ali's appointment as successor before the largest possible audience. This public designation served to affirm a divinely sanctioned line of leadership, integral to the universal principles of Islam.*

- ***Divine Wisdom and Continuity:*** *Numerous narrations indicate that the Prophet (peace be upon him and his family) had been commanded by Allah to announce the Imamate of Amir al-Mu'minin (peace be upon him) publicly. However, he hesitated, aware that some might perceive this act as merely his personal opinion, thus risking rejection of the divine appointment. To fulfill this divine command, he waited for a suitable opportunity where the conditions would support this proclamation. The awaited command was* *confirmed with the revelation of the verse in Surah Al-Ma'idah:*

"O Messenger, convey what has been revealed to you from your Lord; and if you do not, then you have not conveyed His message. And Allah will protect you from the people." (Al-Ma'idah: 67)

- ***Perfection of Islam Through Divine Appointment:*** *The completion of the Islamic message required the appointment of a righteous, divinely appointed leader after the Prophet. This was essential for preserving Islam's universal and eternal mission, with all aspects of the Prophet's role—except for prophethood—transferred to his successor. The verse from Surah Al-Ma'idah, "This day I have perfected for you your religion and completed My favor upon you, and have approved Islam as religion for you" (Al-Ma'idah: 3), was revealed following this proclamation, signifying the perfection and divine completion of Islam with the appointment of Imam Ali.*

- ***Commentary from Sunni and Shia Scholars:*** *Commentators from both Sunni and Shia traditions have documented this event, noting that it took place during the Prophet's Farewell Pilgrimage, mere months before his passing. The verse emphasized that with the appointment of the Prophet's successor,*

Allah's favor was fully realized, and the disbelievers despaired of undermining Islam.

3. The Prophet's Declaration: Key Narrations!

- ***Primary Declaration:*** *During his address, the Prophet held Imam Ali's hand before the crowd and proclaimed, "For whomever I am his Mawla, Ali is his Mawla." He followed this with a call to the gathered assembly to witness and testify to the message. This was a divine appointment, designed to ensure Islam's continuity, with Imam Ali entrusted as the Prophet's immediate successor.*

- ***Witness of Prominent Companions:*** *Among the companions present were notable figures who confirmed the pledge of allegiance to Imam Ali, including Abu Bakr and Umar, with the latter congratulating Imam Ali by saying, "Congratulations, congratulations to you, O Ali! You have become my master and the master of every believing man and woman."*

4. Quranic and Narrational Evidence for Successors After Imam Ali

- **Confirmation of Successive Leadership:** *In a narration by the prominent Sunni scholar Al-Hamawini, it is recorded that Abu Bakr and Umar later asked the Prophet about the specific significance of the verse for Imam Ali. The Prophet confirmed, "Yes, it is for him and for my successors until the Day of Judgment." He proceeded to clarify, saying:*

"Ali is my brother, my minister, my inheritor, my executor, my successor among my people, and the guardian of every believer after me, followed by my son Hasan, then my son Husayn, then nine descendants from Husayn, one after another. The Quran is with them, and they are with the Quran; it will never separate from them, nor they from it, until they return to me at the [heavenly] pond."

5. Theological Implications and the Theme of Universalism vs. Sectarianism

- *Universal Mandate: The event at Ghadir Khumm serves as a clear universal directive, establishing divinely appointed leadership that aligns with Islam's message of unity and guidance. The Prophet's announcement was not merely a matter of family loyalty but a divinely commanded transition of authority that provided the Ummah with a direct line of guidance.*

- **Sectarian Divergence:** *The later deviation from this divine appointment laid the foundation for sectarian divides within Islam, as factions formed around differing interpretations and leadership claims. The universal mandate was thus gradually replaced by alternative models, leading to fragmentation within the Muslim community.*

Incident of Ghadir Khumm: References from Umari Sources

1. Sahih Muslim

- **Volume 4, Book 31, Hadith 5920:** *This narration captures the Prophet's words, "For whomever I am his Mawla, Ali is his Mawla," highlighting the significance of this declaration in the presence of the companions.*

2. Musnad Ahmad ibn Hanbal

- *Volume 4, Page 281: Ahmad ibn Hanbal records the Prophet's declaration at Ghadir Khumm, documenting the explicit statement regarding Imam Ali's guardianship and authority.*

2. Al-Mustadrak by Al-Hakim al-Nishapuri

- *Volume 3, Page 109: Al-Hakim authenticates the hadith of Ghadir Khumm, affirming its credibility and detailing the Prophet's public proclamation, witnessed by thousands, confirming Imam Ali's status as Mawla.*

4. Tafsir al-Tabari

- *Volume 3, Pages 198-199: Tabari's commentary includes accounts from witnesses to the event, with the Prophet's explicit appointment of Imam Ali. Tabari emphasizes this declaration as a formal and divinely mandated designation.*

5. Tafsir Ibn Kathir

- *Volume 4, Page 113: Ibn Kathir references the incident, documenting the Prophet's statement on Imam Ali's guardianship. This tafsir, while sometimes interpreted in a more spiritual than political light, acknowledges the declaration at Ghadir.*

Conclusion.

The Incident at Ghadir Khumm stands as a defining moment in Islamic history, marking the Prophet's clear intention for succession and the continuity of divine guidance after his passing. By publicly declaring, "For whomever I am his Mawla, Ali is his Mawla," the Prophet established a framework for leadership rooted in spiritual purity and unwavering dedication to Islamic principles. This declaration was reinforced by the Quranic verse: "This day I have perfected for you your religion and completed My favor upon you, and have approved Islam as religion for you" (Al-Ma'idah: 3), signifying the divine completion and perfection of Islam through the appointment of Imam Ali.

With Ghadir Khumm, the Prophet intended to unify the Ummah under divinely appointed leadership, aiming to safeguard the universal message of Islam. However, as we transition to the final days of the Prophet's life, the unfolding events reveal a profound divergence from this universal framework. The handling of the Prophet's legacy, especially in his last hours, laid the groundwork for sectarian divisions that would redefine the course of Islamic history. This shift underscores the tension between the Prophet's vision for a unified and guided Ummah and the challenges that arose from competing interpretations and ambitions, ultimately leading to the fragmentation of the community.

In examining the Prophet's final days, we approach a critical juncture where universalism as envisioned at Ghadir Khumm confronts emerging sectarian tendencies. This contrast sets the stage for understanding the lasting impact of the Prophet's life, his message, and the pivotal decisions that followed his departure.

Overview of the Final Hours of the Prophet's Life

1   The Prophet's Final Illness and Call for Companions:

   o *During his final days, the Prophet's health worsened considerably. Recognizing the severity of his illness, he spent much of his time in the home of his wife Aisha, with several key companions frequently visiting him.*

   o *The Prophet reportedly made several requests for close companions to assemble around him, signaling the gravity of his final messages and possibly intending to address succession and guidance. His words during this time focused on preserving unity within the Ummah and adhering strictly to divine guidance.*

3.   The Event of the Pen and Paper:

o *One of the most discussed incidents in Islamic history occurred when the Prophet asked for pen and paper to write a statement that, he said, would prevent the Ummah from straying after his death. This event, known as the "Calamity of Thursday," is marked by significant controversy.*

o *The Prophet's request was met with objections, notably from Umar, who allegedly remarked that the Prophet's illness was affecting his judgment, saying, "The Book of Allah is sufficient for us." This statement resulted in a division among those present, some supporting the Prophet's request and others opposing it. The tension led to the Prophet dismissing them without completing his intended message.*

o *This moment is seen as pivotal, with many scholars interpreting it as a missed opportunity for clear succession, which ultimately led to lasting division within the Ummah.*

3. Prophet's Final Instructions on Prayer and Treatment of the Ansar:

o *In his final hours, the Prophet emphasized the importance of prayer, reminding the Ummah of its centrality to the faith. He also gave specific instructions on the treatment of the Ansar, who had supported him and the Muhajirun (Emigrants) since the early days of Islam.*

o *His statements during these last moments reflected his concerns for the Ummah's future unity and welfare, as well as his desire to see the bonds between various groups preserved and strengthened.*

4. The Prophet's Final Moments and Passing:

o *The Prophet's last moments were spent in a weakened state, reportedly whispering final words that included a prayer or invocation, sometimes described as "O Allah, with the highest companions."*

o *His passing marked the end of his direct leadership, leaving a vacuum that soon led to debates over succession, with factions emerging regarding who should lead the community in his absence.*

5. Immediate Reactions and the Assembly at Saqifah:

o *Following his death, news spread rapidly, and groups quickly convened at Saqifah to discuss the succession. This gathering became a defining moment, as different opinions surfaced regarding the rightful leadership of the Muslim community.*

o *While Ali and other close family members focused on the burial rites, discussions at Saqifah resulted in the selection of Abu Bakr as the first caliph, setting a precedent for succession that would shape the future of Islamic governance.*

Prevention of the Prophet's Last Will to Appoint Ali

- ***Sahih al-Bukhari*** *(Volume 1, Book 3, Hadith 114): In this narration, the Prophet requested writing materials to prevent the Ummah from going astray, but he was met with objections, primarily from Umar, who reportedly said, "The Book of Allah is sufficient for us." This disagreement prevented the Prophet from writing his final instructions, a point of contention that many scholars argue was to clarify succession.*

- ***Musnad Ahmad ibn Hanbal*** *(Volume 1, Page 222): This hadith similarly recounts the Prophet's request for writing materials and the objections from companions present, leading to a division among those who were with him. Ahmad ibn Hanbal's version emphasizes the tension surrounding this request, highlighting it as a missed moment for explicit guidance.*

Awareness of the Prophet's Imminent Passing Due to Poisoning

- ***Sahih al-Bukhari*** *(Volume 5, Book 59, Hadith 713): This narration discusses the Prophet's reflections on the poison he had consumed in Khaybar, expressing that he felt its effects years later. The Prophet's awareness of his imminent death due to poisoning is referenced here, with the Prophet stating that the poison from Khaybar was still affecting him.*

- ***Sahih Muslim*** *(Book 26, Hadith 5430): This hadith further recounts that the Prophet mentioned feeling the lingering effects of the poisoned meat from Khaybar, suggesting that certain companions may have anticipated the timing of his passing.*

Absence of Saqifah Attendees from the Prophet's Burial

- ***Tabaqat Ibn Sa'd*** *(Volume 2, Pages 260-263): This historical source recounts the gathering at Saqifah while the Prophet's family prepared for his burial. Ali, along with the Prophet's close family members, focused on burial rites, while some prominent companions met separately at Saqifah to discuss leadership.*

- ***Tarikh al-Tabari*** *(Volume 3, Pages 198-199): Tabari describes the assembly at Saqifah, detailing that certain figures, including Umar and Abu Bakr, prioritized succession discussions over attendance at the Prophet's burial. This absence at such a critical moment points to the early division regarding leadership priorities.*

The Incident of the Calamity of Thursday and the Question of Poisoning

1. The Calamity of Thursday: Ibn Abbas's Account

- ***Background:*** *In his final days, the Prophet asked for writing materials to dictate a statement that would guide the Ummah and prevent it from straying after his death. This request, narrated by Ibn Abbas and known as the "Calamity of Thursday" (Hadith al-Raziyya), is documented in several Umari sources.*

- ***Hadith of Ibn Abbas:***

  - ***Sahih al-Bukhari*** *(Volume 1, Book 3, Hadith 114): In this narration, Ibn Abbas recounts that the Prophet asked for materials, but Umar objected, suggesting, "The Book of Allah is sufficient for us." This objection led to a division among those present, ultimately resulting in the Prophet's request being denied.*

  - ***Musnad Ahmad ibn Hanbal*** *(Volume 1, Page 222): In Ahmad's narration, Ibn Abbas is deeply pained by the incident, referring to it as a calamity that prevented the Prophet from clearly establishing his final wishes for the Ummah.*

This incident marks a critical moment where the Prophet's intention to clarify succession—many believe to affirm Imam Ali as his successor—was left unfulfilled due to intervention, leading to ambiguity and later division within the Ummah.

2. Claim of Death by Poison from Khaybar

- ***Sunni Account:*** *Many Umari sources claim that the Prophet's death was the result of poisoned meat he ingested during the Battle of Khaybar three years prior. According to these narrations, the Prophet mentioned feeling the lingering effects of the poison as his health declined.*

- ### *Primary Narrations:*

  - ***Sahih al-Bukhari*** *(Volume 5, Book 59, Hadith 713): This hadith recounts that the Prophet reflected on the effects of the poison from Khaybar, suggesting it was still affecting him.*

  - ***Sahih Muslim*** *(Book 26, Hadith 5430): Muslim's narration similarly mentions the Prophet speaking of the poisoned meat from Khaybar as impacting his health in his final days.*

3. Scientific Persective on Poison's Effects

- ***Biological Implausibility****: From a scientific standpoint, it is implausible for a poison ingested three years prior to remain active in the body and cause death so long after. Poisons typically act within hours or days, either being absorbed, expelled, or metabolized by the body. This perspective casts doubt on the narrative attributing the Prophet's death to the Khaybar incident, as no known poison would remain in the system for years without causing immediate fatal effects.*

- ***Alternative Interpretation****: Given these biological limitations, it is possible that the Prophet's death was the result of a more recent poisoning, potentially known to certain companions. The attribution to the Khaybar incident might have been a narrative crafted to distance individuals from responsibility for the Prophet's passing, especially in light of the succession concerns and the "Calamity of Thursday" incident.*

Conclusion and Transition to Post-Prophetic Islam:

The Prophet's final days mark a pivotal moment where explicit guidance on succession was left unrecorded, due to the intervention by certain companions. This incident, coupled with the subsequent gathering at Saqifah during the burial, set the foundation for divisions that would shape Islam's trajectory. The events of these final days underscore a shift from the Prophet's vision of unity under a divinely appointed leader toward competing claims and sectarian divisions that emerged immediately after his passing.

Actions of Abu Bakr and Umar and Their Impact on Division Within the Ummah

1. Forbidding Engagement with the Prophet's Sunnah!

- o *Source: Sahih al-Bukhari (Volume 9, Book 92, Hadith 468)*
- o *Description: Abu Bakr is reported to have discouraged followers from adhering to hadith, focusing solely on the Quran. This aligns with Umar's statement, "The Book of Allah is sufficient for us," implemented as an approach during Abu Bakr's rule.*

2. Burning Hadith Compilations

- o **Source: Al-Khallal, Kitab al-Sunnah** (Volume 1, Page 53)
- o **Description:** *Abu Bakr ordered the burning of hadith compilations in his possession, concerned over potential errors or misuse of the Prophet's sayings.*

3. Seizure of Fadak

- o ***Source: Sahih Muslim*** *(Book 19, Hadith 4351) and **Al-Tabari, Tarikh al-Rusul wal-Muluk** (Volume 1, Page 3193)*
- o ***Description:*** *Following the Prophet's death, Abu Bakr denied inheritance claims by Fatimah, seizing Fadak based on the assertion that prophets leave no inheritance. This action deepened divisions with Ahl al-Bayt.*

4. Attack on Fatimah's House

- o **Source: Al-Baladhuri, Ansab al-Ashraf (Volume 1, Page 586)**
- o ***Description:*** *Abu Bakr ordered Umar to confront those gathered in Fatimah's house, leading to a forceful entry. This incident is cited as a major source of grievance between key companions and the Prophet's family.*

5. Claiming Rights Over Prophet's Assets

- o ***Source: Sunan an-Nasa'i*** *(Volume 5, Book of Estates, Hadith 3371)*
- o ***Description:*** *Abu Bakr assumed control over assets that the Prophet received from believers, sparking disputes over rightful ownership and administration.*

6. Riddah Wars and Killing of Malik Ibn Nuwayrah

- o *Source: Tabari, Tarikh al-Rusul wal-Muluk (Volume 2, Pages 502-504)*
- o ***Description:*** *The Riddah Wars were aimed at consolidating Abu Bakr's control over Arabian tribes. Malik Ibn Nuwayrah's controversial killing during these campaigns intensified divisions and sectarian strife.*

Abu Bakr's Final Confession: Reflections on His Decisions

In his final moments, Abu Bakr reportedly expressed regret over specific actions that he wished he had either refrained from or handled differently:

- o *Source: Tabaqat Ibn Sa'd (Volume 3, Pages 182-185)*

Confession Details: *Abu Bakr confessed three actions he regretted undertaking:*

1. *"I wish I had not exposed the house of Fatimah to anything, even though they had sealed it off for war." This statement reflects regret over the actions taken against Fatimah's house, acknowledging the consequences of this decision.*

2. *"I wish I had not burned the house of the people of al-Silm, and that I had either killed him outright or let him go free." This action, which Abu Bakr viewed as harsh, showcases his doubt over punitive measures he endorsed.*

3. *"I wish that during the Saqifah of Bani Sa'idah, I had placed the matter of leadership around the necks of two men: Umar and*

Abu Ubaydah." He expressed regret over not letting Umar or Abu Ubaydah take leadership instead, reflecting uncertainty over his role in the Saqifah coup.

This confession sheds light on the internal struggles Abu Bakr faced regarding key decisions, revealing the depth of regret over actions that contributed to divisions within the Ummah.

Umar's Role and Actions Diverging from the Prophet's Message

1. Early Incidents of Disagreement During the Prophet's Lifetime

- ### *Treaty of Hudaybiyyah:*

    - *Source: Sahih al-Bukhari (Volume 3, Book 50, Hadith 891)*
    - *Description: During the Treaty of Hudaybiyyah, Umar questioned the Prophet's decision to accept the treaty terms, displaying early resistance to the Prophet's diplomatic approach.*

- ### *The Calamity of Thursday:*

    - *Source: Sahih al-Bukhari (Volume 1, Book 3, Hadith 114)*

- *Description: Umar's statement, "The Book of Allah is sufficient for us," during the Prophet's final days prevented the Prophet's intended guidance from being documented. This intervention had long-lasting effects on the community's unity.*

2. Attack on Fatimah's House and Threat to Burn It

- ### *Threat to Burn the House and Gathering of Wood:*

  - *Source: Al-Baladhuri, Ansab al-Ashraf (Volume 1, Page 586); Ibn Abi Shaybah, al-Musannaf (Volume 8, Page 572)*

  - *Description: Umar, along with supporters, approached Fatimah's house with wood, threatening to burn it if Ali and his supporters did not pledge allegiance to Abu Bakr. Umar's alleged statement, "So what!" in response to being informed of Fatimah's presence exemplifies the harsh measures taken during this period.*

3. Injury to Fatimah and the Miscarriage of Al-Muhsin:

  - *Source: Ibn Qutaybah, Al-Imamah wa al-Siyasah (Volume 1, Pages 12-13)*

- *Description: Umar's forceful entry into Fatimah's house reportedly led to physical harm, pressing her between the door and the wall and allegedly resulting in the miscarriage of her son, Al-Muhsin.*

Hafiz Ibrahim's Poem Praising Umar's Actions:

- *Egyptian poet Hafiz Ibrahim composed a poem honoring Umar, including the line:*

"I will burn your house and leave nothing of it for you, if you do not pledge allegiance, with Az-Zahraa, the daughter of the Chosen One, inside it."

4. Changes in Governance and Policies During His Leadership
   o *Centralization of Authority and Administration:*
     - *Source: Al-Tabari, Tarikh al-Rusul wal-Muluk (Volume 3, Pages 612-615)*
     - *Description: Umar's policies emphasized centralized authority, a marked shift from the Prophet's decentralized approach, which would shape Islamic governance.*

5. Inheritance and Property Rights (Seizure of Fadak):

- *Source: Sahih Muslim (Book 19, Hadith 4351)*
- *Description: Umar upheld Abu Bakr's denial of Fatimah's inheritance to Fadak, reinforcing a policy that diverged from the Prophet's previous practices.*

6. Establishment of the Shura System for Leadership Selection

- *Source: Al-Baladhuri, Ansab al-Ashraf (Volume 5, Page 17)*
- *Description: Umar's establishment of the Shura system for choosing his successor created a model that moved away from the Prophet's lineage-based leadership model, impacting the community's cohesion.*

7. Umar's Reflections in His Final Moments

- *Expressions of Regret and Reflection:*

- *Source 1: Tabaqat al-Kubra - Muhammad ibn Sa'd (Volume 3, Page 360)*
- *Umar expressed profound regret near the end of his life, saying, "I wish I were this piece of hay! I wish I had*

never been created! I wish my mother had never given birth to me! I wish I were nothing! I wish I were forgotten, a lost thing!"

- ■ ***Source 2: Kanuz al-'Amal (Volume 12, Page 619)***
- ■ *In another narration, Umar is recorded as saying, "I wish I were the ram of my family…they would make some of me roasted, some of me salted, then they ate me and expelled me as waste, and I was not human…"*

Conclusion: Islam Between Universalism and Sectarianism

Islam, as established by the Prophet Muhammad, represented a unified, universal message centered on the oneness of God, the prophecy, and the Imamate—culminating in a divine framework intended to guide humanity toward unity, justice, and spiritual fulfillment. During the Prophet's lifetime, his leadership reflected a celestial mandate that emphasized inclusivity, divine guidance, and a familial bond within the Ummah. The message was guided through a clear lineage, with the Prophet appointing Imam Ali at Ghadir Khumm, establishing a universal Islamic governance model rooted in purity and divine knowledge.

However, the period following the Prophet's passing marks a distinct shift from this original vision, as the early companions, led by figures such as Abu Bakr and Umar, instituted policies and practices that diverged from the Prophet's directives. These leaders moved to consolidate authority through human-led decision-making models, prioritizing centralization, allegiance, and political control, as seen in the Saqifah assembly, where allegiance was solidified through forceful means and alternative models of succession were introduced. The actions taken against Ahl al-Bayt—including the seizure of Fadak, the attack on Fatimah's house, and the emphasis on the sufficiency of the Quran over the Sunnah—underscored the stark transition from a divinely led to a human-centered authority, reflecting the rise of sectarianism.

The Differences Between Two Eras

1. Divinely Guided Leadership vs. Human-Centered Governance:

a) *Under the Prophet, leadership was seen as divinely designated, with clear succession plans centered around Imam Ali and Ahl al-Bayt. This structure preserved the unity of the Ummah, providing a leadership rooted in purity and Quranic knowledge.*

b) *Post-Prophetic leadership, however, introduced the Shura system and decisions made by councils, leading to a system where succession was determined by consultation rather than divine appointment, thus fragmenting the original universal message.*

2. Inclusion of Ahl al-Bayt vs. Marginalization:

a) *During the Prophet's life, Ahl al-Bayt held a central position, emphasized through Ayat al-Tathir, which highlighted their purity and their role in preserving the Islamic message.*

b) *After the Prophet, policies of exclusion and opposition against Ahl al-Bayt became prominent. Incidents like the attack on Fatimah's house and the denial of Fadak's inheritance marginalized Ahl al-Bayt, effectively sidelining those whom the Prophet had intended as leaders.*

3. Unity Through Spiritual and Social Guidance vs. Sectarian Divide:

a) *The Prophet's universalism sought to unify people across ethnic and social boundaries, emphasizing collective responsibility and the following of both Quran and Sunnah.*

b) *The post-Prophetic period introduced divisions, focusing on political authority, territorial expansion, and policies that prioritized centralization over unity. This era witnessed the enforcement of the* **Wars of Apostasy (Riddah Wars)** *and the imposition of taxes like the jizya, which divided communities, creating social and economic rifts.*

The Lasting Impact on Islam

The Prophet's model represented Islam's universal mission, with the divine intention of establishing an indivisible faith. His leadership sought to transcend differences, emphasizing the oneness of God, unity within the Ummah, and a divinely appointed lineage to safeguard the faith. However, the subsequent era introduced sectarianism, marking a departure from the initial model. Leadership shifted from a unified, celestial mission to a system characterized by political maneuvering, resulting in diverse interpretations, sects, and ultimately a fractured Islamic identity.

This thesis has highlighted the effects of each era on the integrity of Islam as a celestial message. The Prophet's model emphasized universal values of guidance and unity, while the actions following his death introduced a political dimension, fragmenting the Ummah. Today, the challenge remains to reconcile Islam's universal principles with the sectarian divisions rooted in this historic divergence.

About the Author:

Professor S. Norman G., stands out as a distinguished figure in the field of critical thinking, particularly in its sharp analytical skills, keen observation, and the art of posing essential questions. With his talent, he excels in extracting and developing techniques for creating objective, precise, and possible solutions, avoiding excessive reliance on emotions, and steering clear of selective perception or unconscious bias.

He is a professor of literature, science, and academia, an active and engaging debater, and an expert in Arabic linguistics, morphology, grammar, religious sciences, philosophy, and logic. His intellectual, literary, and doctrinal contributions shine through, merging all sciences under the banner of critical thinking, which is impartial, fair, and unbiased. This approach simplifies understanding the topics he presents with passion and dedication, promoting critical thinking and exploring complex intersections between reason and religious belief systems, especially in the diverse threads of Islamic creeds.

Professor S. Norman G. holds an advanced degree in Social Communication with a specialization in "Critical Thinking." His sharp intelligence is honed through extensive and rigorous academic studies and thorough research in various specialized fields.

In this book, Professor Norman G. focuses on specialists in the science of disagreement or comparative jurisprudence between so-called Islamic sects. His goal is to understand the differing opinions of scholars and appreciate their approaches to Islamic jurisprudence while benefiting from others' experiences to ultimately arrive at what Allah

Almighty desires — not just what is closer to what Allah intended.

For those who do not know what Allah desires, they may accuse Allah and His Messenger of negligence, relying on other than the People of Remembrance (Ahl al-Bayt), who Allah has purified and cleansed thoroughly. Without proper understanding, they will never draw near to Allah.

This inviolable principle, protected by Allah's infallibility, is the foundation for those who seek Allah's guidance. Professor G. builds upon this to construct, coordinate, and refine scientific and rational narratives with solid and convincing analyses. Through this effort, he reaches definitive conclusions backed by compelling evidence.

Professor S. Norman G.'s body of work consists of two main contributions that have garnered wide acceptance and praise. In his first groundbreaking research, *"Ruminating The Past Corrupts Reflection,"* Professor G, addresses the pitfalls of relying on transmission in research, exposing its negative impact on thinking, comprehension, and independent decision-making.

In his second, extensive study, *"Companionship in the Qur'an,"* he sheds light on the deep meanings and connections of love, friendship, and brotherhood found in the Qur'an and other sacred texts, providing intricate insights into the essence of these concepts through the verses of the Qur'an.

Driven by a strong desire to overcome linguistic barriers and reach a diverse audience of various languages and cultures, Professor S. Norman G. has published his works in three languages so far: Arabic, English, and French. Soon, God willing, in Spanish. His commitment to inclusivity underscores his dedication to fostering global dialogue, cultural exchange, and shared understanding.

Professor S. Norman G. continues his journey with insatiable curiosity, forging ahead in his intellectual, literary, and scientific endeavors with unwavering determination. His writings pulse with love, sincerity, and a commitment to guiding others to what is most upright. This book, " *Guided By Light: Between Insight And Rite!*," presents evolved, deep-rooted insights grounded in the eternal and lasting wisdom of the Glorious Qur'an.

Professor G. perseveres in his journey of knowledge and faith, leaving an indelible mark on academic, literary, and religious fields. He consistently offers fresh perspectives, encouraging and motivating readers to engage in constructive and critical examination of their beliefs and the views of their scholars. He promotes intellectual curiosity, openness to others, and a serious commitment to respecting diverse beliefs.

We ask for your prayers!

Indeed,
Allah only
only desires to remove
impurity
O people foth you,
O people on to
and purify you
thoroughly.

Universalism and Secterianism
in Islam

64